Handy Rhode Island Genealogy Handbook

By Gary L. Morris

ISBN-13: 978-1507659182

ISBN-10: 1507659180

Table of Contents

Notes

Genealogical Research in Rhode Island

As one of the original thirteen colonies, there are many historical and genealogical records and resources available for tracing your family history in Rhode Island. Because there are so many records held at many different locations, tracking down the records for your ancestor can be an ominous task. Don't worry though, we know just where they are, and we'll show you which records you'll need, while helping you to understand:

1. What they are
2. Where to find them
3. How to use them

These records can be found both online and off, so we'll introduce you to online websites, indexes and databases, as well as brick-and-mortar repositories and other institutions that will help with your research in Rhode Island. So that you will have a more comprehensive understanding of these records, we have provided a brief history of the "Ocean State" to illustrate what type of records may have been generated during specific time periods. That information will assist you in pinpointing times and locations on which to focus the search for your Rhode Island ancestors and their records.

A Brief History of Rhode Island

The Narragansett and Wampanoag Indians inhabited the area when the first Europeans, an expedition led by Giovanni da Verrazano, explored Rhode Island in 1524. It wasn't until 1636 that the first permanent settlement was established by English clergyman Roger Williams at Providence. The area was popular with those seeking freedom from religious persecution, and many other nonconformist groups established settlements at Portsmouth in 1638, Newport in 1639, and Warwick in 1642.

The four settlements were united into a single colony in 1644, until granted a royal charter by King Charles in 1663. The charter granted religious freedom, self government, and strengthened the territorial claims of the colony. The area became attractive to those seeking freedom from oppression, and many more nonconformists flocked to the area. The ensuing encroachments by white settlers on Native American lands led to and Indian uprising known as King Philip's War (1675–76). The Indians were soundly defeated, and the early part of the following century saw significant growth in agriculture and commerce, including the trading of slaves.

Because of its great degree of self-rule, Rhode Island had much to lose from British attempts at domination of the colonies after 1763. Consequently, in May of 1776, Rhode Island was the first colony to renounce British Rule. Having grown use to a large amount of independence, Rhode Island was hesitant to join the Union, and was the last state to do so, withholding ratification until May 29, 1790.

The 19th century saw urbanization, industrialization, and immigration increasing immensely. Rhode Island's royal charter was still in effect at this time, and there was no procedure in place to amend it. Almost unlimited power was conferred on the legislature through the charter, and it gave disproportionate influence to the declining rural towns. Additionally, suffrage was restricted to estate owners and their eldest sons. This led to a group of political reformers known as the People's Convention moving to bypass the state legislature. Though some resistance was given by a coalition of Whigs and Democrats, a new constitution was implemented in 1843.

Important Dates in Rhode Island History

1636 – First settlement established at Providence

1638 – Settlement founded at Portsmouth

1639 – Settlement established at Newport

1647 – Rhode Island Colony unites with Warwick colony

1657 – First Quakers arrive in Rhode Island

1685 – French Huguenot refugees settle in Rhode Island

1747 – Towns of Tiverton, Warren, Little Compton, and Bristol annexed from Massachusetts

1776 – First colony to renounce British rule

1776 – British army occupies Newport

1779 – British army driven from Newport

1790 – Joins Union

Famous Battles Fought in Rhode Island

King Philip's War of 1675-1676 was the bloodiest conflict of 17th century New England. On a per capita basis, it was the bloodiest war in American history. During the Revolutionary War, the only conflict to take place in the state was the **Battle of Rhode Island**. No Civil War battles took place in the state, but **Rhode Island Regiments** played an important role in several major Civil War conflicts.

These battle accounts that exist can be very effective in uncovering the military records of your ancestor. They can tell you what regiments fought in which battles, and often include the names and ranks of many officers and enlisted men.

King Philip's War:
http://www.historyplace.com/specials/writers/kingphilip.htm

Battle of Rhode Island: http://www.rhodeislandsar.org/battleri.htm

Rhode Island Regiments:
http://www.rihs.org/mssinv/Mss673sg4.htm

Common Rhode Island Genealogical Issues and Resources to Overcome Them

Boundary Changes: Boundary changes are a common obstacle when researching Rhode Island ancestors. You could be searching for an ancestor's record in one county when in fact it is stored in a different one due to historical county boundary changes.

The **Atlas of Historical County Boundaries** can help you to overcome that problem. It provides a chronological listing of every boundary change that has occurred in the history of Rhode Island.

Atlas of Historical County Boundaries:
http://publications.newberry.org/ahcbp/documents/RI_Consolidated_Chronology.htm#Consolidated_Chronology

Name Changes: Surname changes, variations, and misspellings can complicate genealogical research. It is important to check all spelling variations. Soundex, a program that indexes names by sound, is a useful first step, but you can't rely on it completely as some name variations result in different Soundex codes. The surnames could be different, but the first name may be different too. You can also find records filed under initials, middle names, and nicknames as well, so you will need to **get creative with surname variations** and spellings in order to cover all the possibilities. For help with surname variations read our instructional article on **How to Use Soundex**.

get creative with surname variations:
http://obituarieshelp.org/blog/?p=634

How to Use Soundex: http://obituarieshelp.org/blog/?p=505

Rhode Island Genealogical Organizations and Archives

Genealogical resources include not only records, but the organizations that house them, or can direct you to them. These institutions include: *Archives, Libraries, Genealogical Societies, Family History Centers, Universities, Churches, and Museums.*

Following are links to their websites, their physical addresses, and a summary of the records you can find there.

Archives and Libraries

Rhode Island State Archives - state census records, military records, historical newspapers, colonial petitions, and correspondences

337 Westminster St.
Providence, RI 02903
Phone: (401) 222-2353
Fax: (401) 222-3199

Rhode Island State Archives: http://sos.ri.gov/archives/

Providence Public Library - city directories, house directories, family biographies, Arnold's Vital Records and regimental histories of the Civil War

225 Washington St.,
Providence, Rhode Island 02903
Phone: (401) 455-8079

Providence Public Library: http://www.provlib.org/

The National Archives at Boston - Census Records, Naturalization Records, Passenger Arrival Lists, Canadian Border Entry Records, Customs Records, Post-Civil War Tax Records, Draft, Military Service, and Pension and Bounty Land Application Files, Chinese Exclusion Act Case Files, Freedmen's Bureau and Records to African American Families, Dawes Commission Final Cards of the Five Civilized Tribes

380 Trapelo Road
Waltham, Massachusetts
02452-6399
Toll Free Telephone: (866) 406-2379
Telephone: (781) 663-0144
Fax: (781) 663-0154
E-mail: boston.archives@nara.gov

The National Archives at Boston:
http://www.archives.gov/boston/public/genealogy.html

Rhode Island Genealogical and Historical Societies

Genealogical and historical societies have access to extensive catalogues of genealogical data. They are also able to offer expert guidance for genealogical researchers. Many members are professional genealogists who are most willing to share their expertise in finding ancestors.

Rhode Island Historical Society - federal and state census records, historical newspapers, military histories, manuscripts, Revolutionary War and Civil War records, abstracts of deeds, land grants, probate records, genealogies, town records, and cemetery records.

John Brown House
52 Power Street
Providence, RI 02906
Tel: 401.273.7507

Rhode Island Historical Society: http://www.rihs.org/

Rhode Island Genealogical Society - Cemetery Records, Census, Church Records, Family Histories, Passenger Lists, Probate Records, Vital Records

P.O. Box 433
Greenville, RI 02828

Rhode Island Genealogical Society: http://www.rigensoc.org/

Newport Historical Society - church, early town and cemetery records for Newport, manuscript collection with ship logs

82 Touro St.
Newport, RI 02840
Tel (401) 846-0813
Fax (401) 846-1853
Email: info@newporthistorical.org

Newport Historical Society: http://www.newporthistorical.org/

Rhode Island Mailing Lists

Mailing lists are internet based facilities that use email to distribute a single message to all who subscribe to it. When information on a particular surname, new records, or any other important genealogy information related to the mailing list topic becomes available, the subscribers are alerted to it. Joining a mailing list is an excellent way to stay up to date on Rhode Island genealogy research topics. Rootsweb have an extensive listing of **Rhode Island Mailing Lists** on a variety of topics.

Rhode Island Mailing Lists:
http://lists.rootsweb.ancestry.com/index/usa/RI/misc.html

Rhode Island Message Boards

A message board is another internet based facility where people can post questions about a specific genealogy topic and have it answered by other genealogists. If you have questions about a surname, record type, or research topic, you can post your question and other researchers and genealogists will help you with the answer. Be sure to check back regularly, as the answers are not emailed to you. The Rhode Island message boards at **Rootsweb** are completely free to use.

Rhode Island Genealogy Forum link to:
http://boards.rootsweb.com/localities.northam.usa.states/mb.ashx

Rhode Island Newspapers and Periodicals

Many genealogy periodicals and historical newspapers contain
reprinted copies of family genealogies, transcripts of family Bible
records, information about local records and archives, census
indexes, church records, queries, land records, obituaries, court
records, cemetery records, and wills. The following sites have
historical Rhode Island newspapers and periodicals that you can
search online or on-site.

Rhode Island State Archives - microfilms of almost every
newspaper published in Rhode Island from 1732

337 Westminster St.
Providence, RI 02903
Phone: (401) 222-2353
Fax: (401) 222-3199

Rhode Island State Archives: http://sos.ri.gov/archives/

Newport Public Library - Bound volumes of the Newport Daily
News, 1846 -1971, Bound volumes of the Newport Mercury, 1835 -
1965, Microfilm issues of the Newport Daily News, 1846 to present,
Microfilm issues of the Newport Mercury, 1829 -1863, missing
years in the 1840's.

300 Spring Street
Newport, Rhode Island 02840
Telephone: 401-847-8720
FAX: 401-842-0841
Email: info@newportlibraryri.org

Newport Public Library: http://www.newportlibraryri.org/npl/e-
resources/local-history/rhode-island-newspapers/

GenealogyBank.com – free searchable database of Rhode Island newspaper archives, 1732–1921

GenealogyBank.com:
http://www.genealogybank.com/gbnk/newspapers/explore/USA/RhodeIsland/

The Online Books Page – links to historical Rhode Island books and periodicals available for viewing online

The Online Books Page:
http://onlinebooks.library.upenn.edu/webbin/book/browse?type=subject&c=c&key=rhode+island

Library of Congress Digital Newspaper Directory – free searchable database of historical U.S. newspapers dating from 1690-present

Library of Congress Digital Newspaper Directory:
http://chroniclingamerica.loc.gov/search/titles/

NewspaperArchive.com – largest online database of historical newspapers in the world.

NewspaperArchive.com: http://newspaperarchive.com/

Historical Rhode Island Maps and Gazetteers

Maps are an integral part of genealogical research. They help us to locate landmarks, towns, cities, parishes, states, provinces, waterways and roads and streets. They also help us to determine when and where boundary changes might have taken place, and give us a visualization of the area we're researching in.

For locating place names, a gazetteer is the best possible resource for any genealogist. Gazetteers are also sometimes called "place name dictionaries", and can help you to locate the area in which you need to conduct research. Below are links to the maps and gazetteers for research in Rhode Island.

Peabody GNIS Service – Rhode Island
Color Landform Atlas – Rhode Island
1985 U.S. Atlas
Rhode Island Hometown Locator

Peabody GNIS Service – Rhode Island:
http://peabody.research.yale.edu/cgi-bin/Query.GNIS?ST=Rhode%20Island&SU=1

Color Landform Atlas – Rhode Island:
http://fermi.jhuapl.edu/states/ri_0.html

1985 U.S. Atlas: http://www.livgenmi.com/1895/RI/

Rhode Island Hometown Locator:
http://rhodeisland.hometownlocator.com/

Rhode Island City Directories

.

City directories are similar to telephone directories in that they list the residents of a particular area. The difference though is what is important to genealogists, and that is they pre-date telephone directories. You can find an ancestor's information such as their street address, place of employment, occupation, or the name of their spouse. A one-stop-shop for finding city directories in Rhode Island is the **Rhode Island Online Historical Directories** which contains a listing of every available online historical directory related to Rhode Island.

Rhode Island Online Historical Directories: https://sites.google.com/site/onlinedirectorysite/Home/usa/ri

Providence Public Library - Providence City Directories 1827-current

225 Washington St.,
Providence, Rhode Island 02903
Phone: (401) 455-8079

Providence Public Library: http://www.provlib.org/

Rhode Island Genealogical Records

<u>Birth, Death, Marriage and Divorce Records</u> – Also known as vital records, birth, death, and marriage certificates are the most basic, yet most important records attached to your ancestor. The reason for their importance is that they not only place your ancestor in a specific place at a definite time, but potentially connect the individual to other relatives. Below is a list of repositories and websites where you can find Rhode Island vital records.

Rhode Island records of births, marriages, and deaths have been kept by **Town Clerks** since the 1630s

Town Clerks:
http://www.health.ri.gov/records/about/clerkoffices/index.php

Rhode Island Department of Health - Birth and marriage filings less than 100 years old and deaths less than 50 years old

Division of Vital Records
3 Capitol Hill
Providence, RI 02908
Tel: 401-222-2812

Rhode Island Department of Healtho:
http://www.health.ri.gov/programs/vitalrecords/index.php

Rhode Island State Archives - statewide filings of birth and marriage records that are over 100 years old and death records over 50 years old

337 Westminster St.
Providence, RI 02903
Phone: (401) 222-2353
Fax: (401) 222-3199

Rhode Island State Archives: http://sos.ri.gov/archives/

Rhode Island Historical Society – Rhode Island vital records from 1636 to 1920 including births to 1898, marriages to 1900, deaths to 1920, delayed birth records (births not recorded at the time of the birth) from 1846 to1895, with a corresponding index from 1846 to 1898.

John Brown House
52 Power Street
Providence, RI 02906
Tel: 401.273.7507

Rhode Island Historical Society: http://www.rihs.org/

Family Search has the following indexes which can be searched online for free:

Rhode Island, Births and Christenings, 1600-1914:
https://familysearch.org/search/collection/1675525

Rhode Island, Deaths and Burials, 1802-1950:
https://familysearch.org/search/collection/1675536

Rhode Island, Marriages, 1724-1916:
https://familysearch.org/search/collection/1675538

Census Reports

Census records are among the most important genealogical documents for placing your ancestor in a particular place at a specific time. Like BDM records, they can also lead you to other ancestors, particularly those who were living under the authority of the head of household.

Federal census records for Rhode Island exist from 1790 –1930 and can be found at:

Rhode Island State Archives - state census records, 1875-1935

337 Westminster St.
Providence, RI 02903
Phone: (401) 222-2353
Fax: (401) 222-3199

Rhode Island State Archives: http://sos.ri.gov/archives/

The National Archives at Boston – Rhode Island federal census records 1790-1930

380 Trapelo Road
Waltham, Massachusetts
02452-6399
Toll Free Telephone: (866) 406-2379
Telephone: (781) 663-0144
Fax: (781) 663-0154
E-mail: boston.archives@nara.gov

The National Archives at Boston:
http://www.archives.gov/boston/public/genealogy.html

Family Search has the following online indexes which can be searched for free:

Rhode Island, State Census 1835:
https://familysearch.org/search/collection/1529126

Rhode Island, State Census, 1885:
https://familysearch.org/search/collection/1794115

Rhode Island, State Census, 1905:
https://familysearch.org/search/collection/1542866

Rhode Island, State Census, 1915:
https://familysearch.org/search/collection/1532188

Rhode Island, State Census, 1925:
https://familysearch.org/search/collection/1532195

The **Free Census Project** has transcribed many Rhode Island indexes and new material is added daily

Free Census Project: http://usgwcensus.org/cenfiles/ri.htm

Access Genealogy – Rhode Island county census records dating from 1790

Access Genealogy: http://www.accessgenealogy.com/census/rhode-island-census-records.htm

African American Census Schedules Online – slave schedules, mortality schedules, slave-owners census

African American Census Schedules Online:
http://www.afrigeneas.com/aacensus/ga/

Native Americans in Census Records (US National Archives)

Native Americans in Census Records:
http://www.archives.gov/research/census/native-americans/

Rhode Island Church Records

Church and synagogue records are a valuable resource, especially for baptisms, marriages, and burials that took place before 1900. You will need to at least have an idea of your ancestor's religious denomination, and in most cases you will have to visit a brick and mortar establishment to view them.

Most church records are kept by the individual church, although in some denominations, records are placed in a regional archive or maintained at the diocesan level. Local Historical Societies are sometimes the repository for the state's older church records. Below are links archives that maintain church records, as well as a few databases that can be viewed online.

The **Family History Library** contains many church records from a variety of denominations on microfilm.

Family History Library:
http://familysearch.org/learn/wiki/en/Family_History_Library

Central Repositories for Denominational Records

Church of Jesus Christ of Latter-day Saints (Mormons)

Early Mormon Church records for Rhode Island can be found on film located at the LDS Family History Library in Salt Lake City and can be searched via the **Family History Library Catalog**

Family History Library Catalog:
https://familysearch.org/eng/Library/FHLC/frameset_fhlc.asp

Baptist

American Baptist Historical Society
3001 Mercer University Dr
Atlanta, GA 30341
Telephone: (678) 547-6680

American Baptist Historical Society: http://abhsarchives.org/

Congregational

The Congregational Library
14 Beacon Street
Boston, MA 02108-3704
Phone: (617) 523-0470
Fax: (617) 523-0491

The Congregational Library: http://www.14beacon.org/

Episcopal

Diocese of Connecticut
135 Asylum Avenue
Hartford, CT 06105-2295
Phone: (860) 233-4481
Fax: (860) 523-1410

Diocese of Connecticut: http://www.ctepiscopal.org/default.asp

Reformed

Sacred Journey Church of Providence, Rhode Island
91 Fricker St.
Providence, RI
Phone: (401) 484-0752

Sacred Journey Church of Providence, Rhode Island:
http://sjchurch.org/

Methodist

Boston University Theological School Library
745 Commonwealth Avenue
Boston, MA 02215
Phone: (617) 353-3034
Fax: (617) 353-3061

Boston University Theological School Library:
http://www.bu.edu/sthlibrary/

United Methodist Archives Center
Drew University Library
P.O. Box 127
Madison, NJ 07940
Phone: (201) 408-3189
Fax: (201) 408-3909

United Methodist Archives Center:
http://www.gcah.org/site/pp.aspx?c=ghKJI0PHIoE&b=3590193

Roman Catholic

Diocese of Providence
The Chancery Office
34 Fenner Street
Providence, RI 02903-3695
Phone: (401) 278-4500
Fax: (401) 278-4548

Diocese of Providence: http://www.dioceseofprovidence.org/

Rhode Island Military Records

More than 40 million Americans have participated in some time of war service since America was colonized. The chance of finding your ancestor amongst those records is exceptionally high. Military records can even reveal individuals who never actually served, such as those who registered for the two World Wars but were never called to duty.

Below are a number of links to websites and archives that contain Rhode Island military records.

Rhode Island Historical Society – Huge collection of Revolutionary War and Civil War records including Continental and state regiments, county militia regiments, court martial proceedings, supply and pay requests, muster rolls, pay rolls and abstracts, enlistments, delinquent lists, returns of the sick, ration bills, and more

John Brown House
52 Power Street
Providence, RI 02906
Tel: 401.273.7507

Rhode Island Historical Society: http://www.rihs.org/

The National Archives at Boston - records from the Revolutionary War, War of 1812, Civil War, Naval Records, and Pension Indexes

380 Trapelo Road
Waltham, Massachusetts
02452-6399
Toll Free Telephone: (866) 406-2379
Telephone: (781) 663-0144
Fax: (781) 663-0154
E-mail: boston.archives@nara.gov

The National Archives at Boston:
http://www.archives.gov/boston/public/genealogy.html

US Department of Veterans Affairs Nationwide Gravesite Locator – includes information on veterans and their family members buried in veterans and military cemeteries having a government grave marker.

US Department of Veterans Affairs Nationwide Gravesite Locator: http://gravelocator.cem.va.gov/

You may also find your ancestor's military records in the following databases:

United States General Index to Pension Files, 1861-1934: https://familysearch.org/search/collection/1919699

United States Index to Service Records, War with Spain, 1898: https://familysearch.org/search/collection/1919583

United States Index to Indian Wars Pension Files, 1892-1926 – military pension records of soldiers who fought in the Indian Wars between 1817 and 1898

United States Index to Indian Wars Pension Files, 1892-1926: https://familysearch.org/search/collection/1979427

United States Registers of Enlistments in the U.S. Army, 1798-1914 - index of men who enlisted in the United States Army, 1798-1914.

United States Registers of Enlistments in the U.S. Army, 1798-1914 : https://familysearch.org/search/collection/1880762

United States Mexican War Pension Index, 1887-1926: https://familysearch.org/search/collection/1979390

Civil War Soldiers Service Records - Service records for both Union and Confederate soldiers indexed by soldier's name, rank, and unit.

Civil War Soldier Service Records: http://go.fold3.com/civilwar_records/

Rhode Island Cemetery Records

As convenient as it is to search cemetery records online, keep in mind that there are a few disadvantages over visiting a cemetery in person. They are:

- Tombstone information is not always accurately transcribed
- The arrangement of the graves in a cemetery can be crucial as family members are often buried next to each other or in the same grave. This arrangement is not always preserved in the alphabetical indexes that are found online.

With that information in mind, the following websites have databases that can be searched online for Rhode Island Cemetery records.

Rhode Island Historical Society – variety of county cemetery records

John Brown House
52 Power Street
Providence, RI 02906
Tel: 401.273.7507

Rhode Island Historical Society: http://www.rihs.org/

Rhode Island Genealogical Society - Cemetery Records from various denominations from around the state

P.O. Box 433
Greenville, RI 02828

Rhode Island Genealogical Society: http://www.rigensoc.org/

Newport Historical Society - church and cemetery records for Newport

82 Touro St.
Newport, RI 02840
Tel (401) 846-0813
Fax (401) 846-1853
Email: info@newporthistorical.org

Newport Historical Society: http://www.newporthistorical.org/

Rhode Island Tombstone Transcription Project - death and burial records

Rhode Island Tombstone Transcription Project:
http://www.usgwtombstones.org/rhodeisland/rho-isl.html

African American Cemeteries Online – African American, slave, and Native American cemetery records

African American Cemeteries Online:
http://africanamericancemeteries.com/ar/

Access Genealogy – database of Rhode Island cemetery record transcriptions

Access Genealogy:
http://www.accessgenealogy.com/cemetery/rhode-island-cemetery-records.htm

Find a Grave – over 100 million grave records can be searched on this site. Search can be conducted by name, location, or cemetery name.

Find a Grave: http://www.findagrave.com/

Interment.net - A free online database containing approximately 4 million cemetery records from around the world.

Interment.net: http://www.interment.net/

Billion Graves – as the name implies, you can search a billion records including headstone photos, transcriptions, cemetery records, and grave locations.

Billion Graves:
http://billiongraves.com/pages/search/index.php#cemetery

Rhode Island Obituaries

Obituaries can reveal a wealth about our ancestor and other relatives. You can search our **Rhode Island Obituaries Listings** from hundreds of Rhode Islandnewspapers online for free.

Rhode Island Obituaries Listings:
http://obituarieshelp.org/rhode_island_newspaper_obituaries.html

Rhode Island Wills and Probate Records

The documents found in a probate packet may include a complete inventory of a person's estate, newspaper entries, witness testimony, a copy of a will, list of debtors and creditors, names of executors or trustees, names of heirs. They can not only tell you about the ancestor you're currently researching, but lead to other ancestors.

Rhode Island Historical Society – probate records and/or wills for many Rhode Island cities and towns dating from the 17th century to the mid-19th century.

John Brown House
52 Power Street
Providence, RI 02906
Tel: 401.273.7507

Rhode Island Historical Society: http://www.rihs.org/

New England Historic Genealogical Society - searchable online catalog of Rhode Island probate records

101 Newbury Street
Boston, Massachusetts 02116, USA
888-296-3447

New England Historic Genealogical Society:
http://library.nehgs.org/

Rhode Island Immigration and Naturalization Records

The naturalization process generated many types of records, including petitions, declarations of intention, and oaths of allegiance. These records can provide family historians with information such as a person's birth date and place of birth, immigration year, marital status, spouse information, occupation, witnesses' names and addresses, and more.

The National Archives at Boston - Rhode Island naturalizations 1842-1991, Providence, RI Passenger lists 1820-1867; 1911-1943, all Atlantic East Coast Port arrivals, 1820-1943, Crew Lists

380 Trapelo Road
Waltham, Massachusetts
02452-6399
Toll Free Telephone: (866) 406-2379
Telephone: (781) 663-0144
Fax: (781) 663-0154
E-mail: boston.archives@nara.gov

The National Archives at Boston:
http://www.archives.gov/boston/public/genealogy.html

Rhode Island Historical Society - collection of passenger lists and passenger list indexes including: Filby's Passenger and Immigration Lists Index, Rhode Island Passenger Lists: Port of Providence, 1798-1808; 1820-1872, Port of Bristol and Warren 1820-1871, Passenger Arrivals at the Port of Providence, 1912-1943, The Great Migration Begins: Immigrants to New England, 1620-(ongoing), The Famine Immigrants: Lists of Irish Immigrants Arriving at the Port of New York, 1846-1851
Passengers to America: A Consolidation of Ship Passenger Lists from the New England Historic Genealogical Register

Rhode Island Historical Society: http://www.rihs.org/immigration-and-naturalization/

Rhode Island Native American Records

The National Archives at Boston - Dawes Commission Final Cards of the Five Civilized Tribes

380 Trapelo Road
Waltham, Massachusetts
02452-6399
Telephone: (781) 663-0144
Fax: (781) 663-0154
E-mail: boston.archives@nara.gov

The National Archives at Boston:
http://www.archives.gov/boston/public/genealogy.html

Access Genealogy – Rhode Island Native American census records, tribal histories, and much more

Access Genealogy: http://www.accessgenealogy.com/native/rhode-island-indian-tribes.htm

U.S. National Archives - information on American Indians who maintained their ties to Federally-recognized Tribes (1830-1970).

U.S. National Archives: http://www.archives.gov/research/native-americans/

Records of the Bureau of Indian Affairs (BIA):
http://www.archives.gov/research/guide-fed-records/groups/075.html

American Indians Records Repository - records dating from the 1700s including trust, education and other historic Indian Affairs records

American Indian Records Repository
Meritex Enterprises
17501 West 98th Street
Lenexa, KS 66219
Phone: 913-888-0601

American Indians Records Repository link to:
http://www.doi.gov/ost/records_mgmt/american-indian-records-repository.cfm

Missing Matriarchs – Resources for Researching Female Rhode Island Ancestors

Looking for female ancestors requires an adjustment of how we view traditional records sources. A woman's identity was often under that of her husband, and often individual records for them can be difficult to locate. The following resources are effective in locating female ancestors in Rhode Island where traditional records may not reveal them.

Bibliographies

- *Genealogical Dictionary of Rhode Island,* John D. Austin (Genealogical Publishing Co., 1984)
- *From Working Daughters to Working Mothers: Immigrant Women in a New England Industrial Community,* Louise Lamphere (Cornell University Press, 1987)
- *Let Virtue Be a Guide to Thee: Needlework in the Education of Rhode Island Women, 1730-1830,* Betty Ring (Rhode Island State Historical Society, 1983)

Selected Resources for Rhode Island Women's History

Rhode Island Historical Society
John Brown House
52 Power Street
Providence, RI 02906
Tel: 401.273.7507

John Hay Library
Brown University
20 Prospect St.
Providence, RI 02912

Common Rhode Island Surnames

The following surnames are among the most common in Rhode Island and are also being currently researched by other genealogists. If you find your surname here, there is a chance that some research has already been performed on your ancestor.

Acker, Anna, Anusewski, Atwater, Babcock, Bailey, Ball, Barker, Barrett, Beckett, Belanger, Bennett, Bergeron, Bissonette, Bliss, Booth, Boswell, Bounty, Bradley, Breck, Brewin, Briggs, Brown, Bucket, Budnitz, C.Roc, Cadieux, Caldorado, Callie, Canady, Carlson, Caron, Castleton, Charbonneau, Charles, Chartier, Chase, Colwes, Cook, Couillard, Couillaud, Crawford, Cunningham, Curley, DeLaPorte, deMarcilly, Desel, Deslaurier, Deved, Diesel, Dorothea, Downs, Dragon, Dragoon, Duchesne, Dumas, Edwards, Eldred, Elizabeth, Emma, Favreau, Favreaux, Fell, Finlayson, Fisher, Francone, Frank, Gauthier, George, Gervais, Gonzalez, Gorton, Greta, Guild, Guntner, H.Pearse, Haden, Hadens, Haldane, Halstead, Hardy, Hartman, Harvey, Haskell, Hatswell, Henley, Herman, Hermann, Horton, Houle, House, Hurley, Hyland, J.Dolan, J.Morgan, Joudin, Judy, Karydis, Keesing, Kenney, Kyle, Labombard, LaFauci, Laforce, Lamson, Lantry, LaRoc, LaRocque, Larsen, Larson, L'Ecuyer, Ledoux, Lippincott, Loveday, Lowther, Lupton, Lyons, MacComb, Mahoney, Maillot, Maloney, Margaret, Marten, Martin, Mary, Matthews, Mayette, McNeil, Menzie, Mercier, Michelle, Mosher, Mundorf, Murray, Nansel, Nolan, Otten, Ouimet, P.T.Hatswell, Pain, Paine, Paine2, Perry, Pierce, Piligian, Powers, Primo, Provost, Prue, Quinn, Rcquebrune, Ream, Reed, Remington, Rendeau, Rice, Riley, Riviere, Roach, Rock, Rooney, Ryan, Sabourin, Sadlo, Sawyer, Seleurier, Sellers, Seward, Shackett, Shaw, Sheldon, Shepherd, Sherman, Sherwood, Signor, Silver, Simmons, Slocum, Smith, Soule, St.Georges, Steele, Sturdy, Sullivan, Sylvester, Taglierini, Terry, Thomas, Tyson, Vose, Wallace, Watson, White, Whiteside, Wilcox, Williams, Winslow, Wodjenski

About the Author

Gary L. Morris worked from 2009 to 2014 as a professional researcher for a major player in the genealogy field. After tracing his family lineage back to 1683, he found that genealogy could be an expensive undertaking. As such, has decided to publish these helpful guides to share the valuable free information he has discovered during his career to help others trace their family lineages as inexpensively as possible. An avid genealogist himself, he hopes you will find this guide factual, thorough, helpful, and most of all, effective in helping you to find your family members.

Notes

Notes